CONNECTICUT

The Constitution State

BY
JOHN HAMILTON

Abdo & Daughters

An imprint of Abdo Publishing | abdopublishing.com

abdopublishing.com

Published by ABDO Publishing, a division of ABDO, PO Box 398166, Minneapolis, Minnesota 55439. Copyright © 2017 by Abdo Consulting Group, Inc. International copyrights reserved in all countries. No part of this book may be reproduced in any form without written permission from the publisher. ABDO & Daughters™ is a trademark and logo of ABDO Publishing.

Printed in the United States of America, North Mankato, Minnesota.
012016
092016

Editor: Sue Hamilton   **Contributing Editor:** Bridget O'Brien
Graphic Design: Sue Hamilton
Cover Art Direction: Candice Keimig   **Cover Photo Selection:** Neil Klinepier
Cover Photo: iStock
Interior Images: Alamy, AP, Bradley International Airport, Bridgeport Sound Tigers, Connecticut Sun, Connecticut Whale, Corbis, Dreamstime, Dr. Macro, Eigenes Werk, George W. Bush Presidential Library & Museum, General Dynamics Electric Boat, Getty, Glow, Granger, Gunter Küchler, Hartford Wolf Pack, History in Full Color-Restoration/Colorization, iStock, Library of Congress, Mile High Maps, NASA, New Britain Rock Cats, New England Black Wolves, Prudence Crandall Museum Collections-Dept of Economic & Community Dev-State of Connecticut, RavenFire Media, Science Source, Techbint, U.S. Fish & Wildlife Service, U.S. Navy Memorial Foundation, Univ. of Connecticut-Huskies, Univ. of Wisconsin-Milwaukee, & Wikimedia.

Statistics: *State and City Populations*, U.S. Census Bureau, July 1, 2014 estimates; *Land and Water Area*, U.S. Census Bureau, 2010 Census, MAF/TIGER database; *State Temperature Extremes*, NOAA National Climatic Data Center; *Climatology and Average Annual Precipitation*, NOAA National Climatic Data Center, 1980-2015 statewide averages; *State Highest and Lowest Points*, NOAA National Geodetic Survey.

Websites: To learn more about the United States, visit booklinks.abdopublishing.com. These links are routinely monitored and updated to provide the most current information available.

Cataloging-in-Publication Data

Names: Hamilton, John, 1959- author.
Title: Connecticut / by John Hamilton.
Description: Minneapolis, MN : Abdo Publishing, [2016] | The United States of America | Includes index.
Identifiers: LCCN 2015957507 | ISBN 9781680783094 (print) | ISBN 9781680774139 (ebook)
Subjects: LCSH: Connecticut--Juvenile literature.
Classification: DDC 974.6--dc23
LC record available at http://lccn.loc.gov/2015957507

CONTENTS

THE CONSTITUTION STATE

Connecticut is a small state with big ambition. Great wealth and industry are found within its compact borders. Bustling cities welcome all kinds of businesses, from insurance companies to factories. Ivy League Yale University is one of the best schools in the nation.

Connecticut also has natural beauty and New England charm. Rolling hills are filled with forests of oak, hickory, and maple trees. Family farms contain stone walls dating back to the state's colonial ancestors. The countryside is dotted with quaint towns built around village greens and white-steepled churches. The state's maritime history is on display at shoreline beaches and ocean port towns.

Connecticut's nickname is "The Constitution State." It was the first American colony to use democratic laws to unite its citizens. This model of self-governance was later used by America's Founding Fathers to help them write the United States Constitution.

The Chester-Hadlyme Ferry carries visitors across the Connecticut River. It is a state historical landmark.

A covered bridge spans a brook at
Connecticut's Chatfield Hollow State Park.

QUICK FACTS

Name: "Connecticut" is from a Mohegan Native American word, *quinnehtukqut*, which means "beside the long tidal river." It refers to the Connecticut River.

State Capital: Hartford, population 124,705

Date of Statehood: January 9, 1788 (5th state)

Population: 3,596,677 (29th-most populous state)

Area (Total Land and Water): 5,543 square miles (14,356 sq km), 48th-largest state

Largest City: Bridgeport, population 147,612

Nickname: The Constitution State

Motto: *Qui Transtulit Sustinet* (He Who Transplanted Still Sustains)

State Bird: American Robin

State Flower: Mountain Laurel

State Mineral: Almandine Garnet

State Tree: Charter Oak (White Oak)

State Song: "Yankee Doodle"

Highest Point: South slope of Mount Frissell, 2,380 feet (725 m)

Lowest Point: Long Island Sound, 0 feet (0 m)

Mount Frissell

Average July High Temperature: 83°F (28°C)

Record High Temperature: 106°F (41°C), in Torrington on August 23, 1916, and Danbury on July 15, 1995

Long Island Sound

Average January Low Temperature: 17°F (-8°C)

Low Temperature: -32°F (-36°C), in Falls Village on February 16, 1943, and in Coventry on January 22, 1961

Average Annual Precipitation: 49 inches (124 cm)

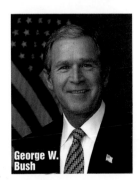

George W. Bush

Number of U.S. Senators: 2

Number of U.S. Representatives: 5

U.S. Presidents Born in Connecticut: George W. Bush (43rd president)

U.S. Postal Service Abbreviation: CT

QUICK FACTS

GEOGRAPHY

Connecticut is the third-smallest state in the United States. It is located in the northeast corner of the country, in a region called New England. Connecticut is the southernmost state in New England. The state is shaped roughly like a rectangle, with a small panhandle in the southwest corner that extends into neighboring New York.

Connecticut shares its western border with New York. Massachusetts is to the north. Rhode Island is to the east. An extension of the Atlantic Ocean called Long Island Sound makes up the southern edge of Connecticut. The state covers 5,543 square miles (14,356 sq km).

The Housatonic River runs through the central western part of Connecticut.

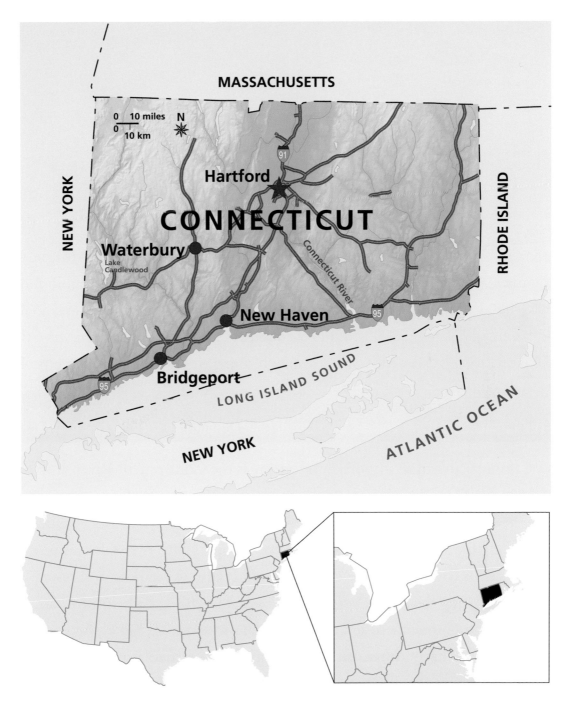

Connecticut's total land and water area is 5,543 square miles (14,356 sq km). It is the 48th-largest state. The state capital is Hartford.

The Connecticut River divides the state of Connecticut into roughly two halves.

Connecticut's most important waterway is the Connecticut River. It is the longest river in New England. It measures 410 miles (660 km) from its source near Canada. It flows southward through Connecticut and empties into Long Island Sound. It divides the state roughly into two halves. The Connecticut River used to be very polluted because of factories and sewer runoffs. During the last 40 years, the water quality has greatly improved.

Although Connecticut is small, it has many people. It has a population of 3,596,677. Early American settlers came here because it was a good location for fishing and trading. It also has good soil for farming. Along the coast and central valley of the Connecticut River, the land is mostly flat. This accounts for about two-thirds of the state. It is where the busiest cities are located.

The northeast and northwest parts of Connecticut are covered in rolling hills. The highest altitudes are found in the northwest. The southern slope of Mount Frissell is the highest point in the state, at 2,380 feet (725 m). However, the mountain's summit is in neighboring Massachusetts. The highest summit contained within Connecticut's borders is nearby Bear Mountain. It is 2,322 feet (708 m) high.

Connecticut's largest lake is Lake Candlewood. It is on the western edge of the state, and covers 8.4 square miles (21.8 sq km).

Man-made Candlewood Lake is bordered by five towns: Brookfield, Danbury, New Fairfield, New Milford, and Sherman, Connecticut. It is a popular recreational area.

CLIMATE AND
WEATHER

Connecticut's climate is mild compared to most of New England, thanks to the moderating waters of the Atlantic Ocean. The state's residents enjoy warm summers, with farmers taking advantage of a long growing season and moderate rainfall. In an average year, there are only 12 days when the temperature rises above 90°F (32°C).

Spring and autumn are very pleasant in Connecticut. Beautiful fall colors blanket the hillsides, thanks to hardwood forests of oak, hickory, and maple trees. Many visitors travel to the state in October and November.

Connecticut has cool winters that aren't too harsh. The thermometer drops below 0°F (-18°C) only six days each year on average. Temperatures in the northern hills are usually colder. Normal snowfall ranges from about 20 inches (51 cm) along the coast, up to 60 inches (152 cm) in the northwestern hills.

Fairfield, Connecticut, deals with one of the state's biggest storms in February 2013. The blizzard dumped 3 feet (.9 m) of snow across Connecticut.

Lightning strikes downtown
New London, Connecticut.

Hurricanes can sometimes lash Connecticut, but thunderstorms are much more common. About 30 storms strike the state each summer. Tornadoes occasionally threaten the Connecticut River Valley.

PLANTS AND ANIMALS

Connecticut has several kinds of habitats that provide wildlife with food, water, and shelter. About 60 percent of the state is forested. Open areas include fields and wetlands. Connecticut has more than 98 miles (158 km) of coastline, including sandy beaches and salt marshes. The center of Connecticut contains a special habitat called a traprock ridge. Steep ridges are either dry and sunny or shady and cool, providing homes for many kinds of plants and animals.

Common animals in Connecticut include rabbits, chipmunks, squirrels, muskrats, otters, white-tailed deer, opossums, foxes, skunks, coyotes, bats, and woodchucks. Beavers thrive in the state's marshes. They like to make dams in slow-moving streams. Fishers are members of the weasel family. These forest animals prefer to make their dens in the hollows of old trees. They, along with black bears, were once hunted so much that they disappeared from Connecticut. Today, both species are making a comeback.

Fisher

A white-tailed deer stands poised to run at Sherwood Island State Park on the shore of Long Island Sound in Westport, Connecticut. Sherwood Island State Park is Connecticut's oldest state park, with the first parcel of land purchased in 1914.

PLANTS AND ANIMALS

A great blue heron wades in Eightmile River at Southford Falls State Park, in Oxford, Connecticut.

There are almost 300 species of birds regularly found in Connecticut. Commonly seen are blue jays, woodpeckers, sparrows, goldfinches, chickadees, red-tailed hawks, owls, ruby-throated hummingbirds, and crows. Game birds include pheasants, ducks, and grouse. Along Connecticut's shores are found anhingas, great blue herons, storm-petrels, cormorants, gulls, and sandpipers.

Wild turkeys are good fliers. They live mostly in Connecticut's forests, but are also found in cornfields and pastures. They feed on berries and acorns, and like to roost in trees at night. Canada geese stay in Connecticut all year long. Some flocks migrate through the state, flying overhead in "V" formations. Connecticut's state bird is the American robin. This songbird is easily spotted by it reddish-orange breast.

Swimming in Connecticut's freshwater rivers and lakes are perch, brook trout, smallmouth bass, northern pike, bullhead, perch, and walleye. Lurking in the waters of Long Island Sound are Atlantic cod, striped bass, flounder, butterfish, and bluefish. The official state shellfish is the eastern oyster. Connecticut's state animal is the sperm whale. It reflects the state's maritime heritage.

Common Connecticut shrubs and bushes include huckleberry, sweet fern, blueberry, and wild cherry. Colorful wildflowers include cowslip, jack-in-the-pulpit, violet, and bloodroot. Mountain laurel is the official state flower. White oak is the state tree.

Salt marsh pink are tiny flowers growing in Connecticut's Stewart B. McKinney National Wildlife Refuge. They live on open, sandy soils.

PLANTS AND ANIMALS

HISTORY

Before Europeans arrived in the early 1600s, Native Americans lived in the land we now call Connecticut. They included the Quiripi, Mohegan, Pequot, Nipmuc, Mahican, and Munsee people, plus several others. They were all

The original Algonquian-speaking Native Americans of Connecticut.

Algonquian-speaking people, but they controlled their own territories. They hunted, fished, and grew crops such as corn, squash, and pumpkins. The name "Connecticut" comes from a Mohegan word that means "beside the long tidal river." It refers to the Connecticut River.

In 1614, Dutch explorer Adriaen Block sailed partway up the Connecticut River. Later, the Dutch built a fur trading post near the present-day city of Hartford.

The first permanent European settlers arrived in 1633. Three years later, in 1636, a large group of English Puritans settled in the Hartford area. Led by Thomas Hooker, they were Puritans from England's neighboring Massachusetts Bay Colony. They were looking for room to farm. Hooker became known as the "Father of Connecticut." The Dutch lost interest in Connecticut as more and more English settlers arrived. Several settlements were combined into one Connecticut Colony.

In 1636,
Thomas Hooker
led English Puritan settlers
to the Hartford, Connecticut, area.

In May 1637, Captain John Mason led English colonists in a war against the Native American Pequots near Stonington, Connecticut.

Connecticut's European settlers had an uneasy relationship with their Native American neighbors. The powerful Pequot people of eastern Connecticut were especially angry. They wanted to control the fur trade, and they wanted the settlers to stop taking Pequot land. Fights broke out. The Pequot began killing traders and settlers. The settlers responded with the Pequot War of 1636 to 1637. Hundreds of Pequot were either killed by colonists or enslaved by enemy tribes.

As life grew more complicated for the English settlers, they decided they needed a better government. Thanks to encouragement by Thomas Hooker, the colonists wrote a new set of laws in 1639. They were called the Fundamental Orders. These laws said that the people of Connecticut had the right to elect their own leaders. Citizens also gained the right to limit government power. These were new ideas that would later be important during the American Revolution.

In the 1700s, tension grew high between England and its American colonies. The colonies declared independence in 1776. During the American Revolutionary War, Connecticut soldiers fought in many important battles. Connecticut also provided guns and other material. George Washington called Connecticut "The Provision State" because of all the supplies given to his army.

After America won independence, representatives from Connecticut helped write the United States Constitution. Connecticut became the fifth state to join the United States on January 9, 1788.

Founding Fathers Benjamin Franklin, John Adams, and Thomas Jefferson read a draft of the Declaration of Independence in 1776.

Cannons are manned by soldiers of the 1st Connecticut Heavy Artillery during the Civil War.

In the early 1800s, Connecticut businesses grew. Farms, textile mills, and busy seaports brought money to the state. Slavery was abolished in 1848. Connecticut soldiers fought for the Union during the American Civil War of 1861–1865. The state contributed more than 50,000 troops to help defeat the southern Confederacy. Many Connecticut factories made weapons. These companies included Pratt & Whitney, New Haven Arms Company, and Colt's Manufacturing Company, which provided many pistols and rifles to Union troops.

In the early 1900s, Connecticut's industry continued to expand. Railroads crisscrossed the state. Factories produced many needed goods, such as metal products, brassware, clocks, and other items. When World War I began in 1914, Connecticut became a major U.S. military supplier. The state also supported the war effort when the United States entered and fought in World War II from 1941 to 1945. Companies such as Winchester Repeating Arms supplied firearms. Connecticut factories also built submarines, aircraft parts, and parachutes.

After World War II, Connecticut made efforts to diversify its economy. Instead of relying on the defense industry, the state began attracting companies that made consumer goods such as sewing machines, jet engines, and motors. Many insurance companies now make Connecticut their headquarters. Tourism has also boomed, with many resorts being built along the state's Long Island Sound shoreline.

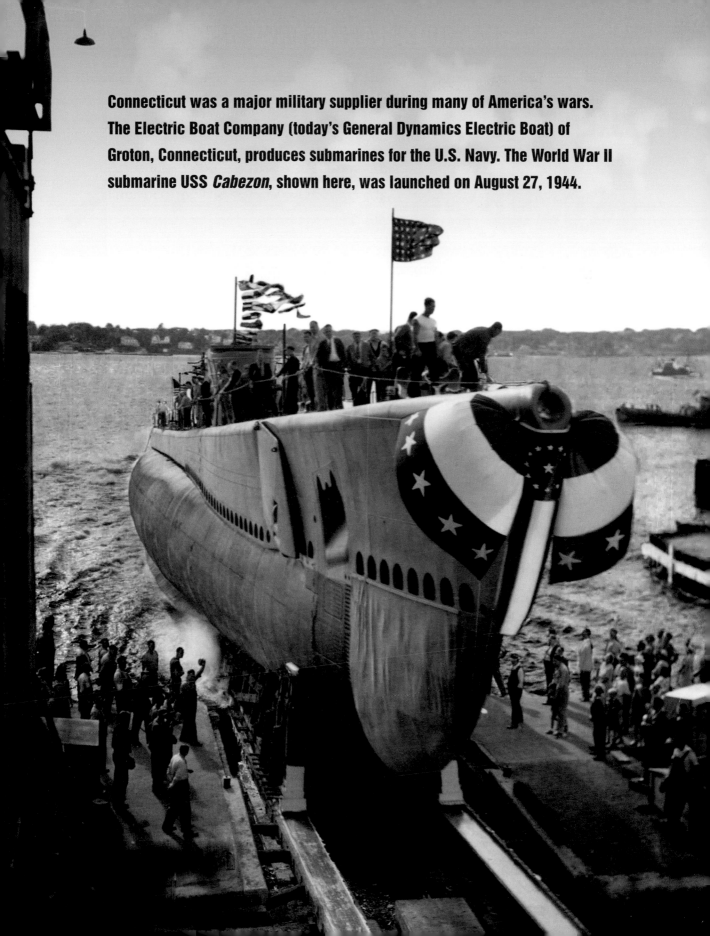

Connecticut was a major military supplier during many of America's wars. The Electric Boat Company (today's General Dynamics Electric Boat) of Groton, Connecticut, produces submarines for the U.S. Navy. The World War II submarine USS *Cabezon*, shown here, was launched on August 27, 1944.

DID YOU KNOW?

- Connecticut's official nickname is "The Constitution State," but many people call it "The Nutmeg State." Why are people from Connecticut nicknamed Nutmeggers? The answer is unclear. Nutmeg is a spice used in cooking. The egg-shaped seeds come from a tropical tree. Early Connecticut traders may have sold the seeds to eager buyers in Europe and elsewhere.

- New Haven, Connecticut, has the largest collection of preserved human brains on display in the United States. The 550 specimens were collected by neurosurgeon Dr. Harvey Cushing (1869-1939) over 30 years for his research in brain surgery. The brains are stored in glass jars at the Harvey Cushing/John Hay Whitney Medical Library at Yale Medical School.

- The town of Rocky Hill, Connecticut, has one of the largest collections of dinosaur tracks in the United States. Found by construction workers in 1966, the site has more than 2,000 tracks. It became Dinosaur State Park in 1968. Today, a geodesic dome covers a group of 500 of the three-toed *Dilophosaurus* tracks.

- By 1662, Connecticut was ruled by a set of laws called the Connecticut Charter. It was a constitution that gave the colony limited self-government. In 1687, the British demanded that Connecticut give up its charter. Governor Robert Treat refused. To protect the document from British troops, it was hidden in the hollow of a massive white oak near Hartford. Even though the 200-year-old tree later blew down in a storm in 1856, the "Charter Oak" remains Connecticut's state tree. It is featured on the Connecticut quarter.

Roger Sherman

- When America's Founding Fathers sat down in 1787 to draft a constitution, they had a big problem. How should the states be represented in the new country? The big states wanted more power. The small states wanted to be represented equally. Lawmakers from Connecticut, including statesman Roger Sherman, had a solution. It was called the Connecticut Compromise. Congress would be split in two: the Senate and the House of Representatives. Each state would have two senators, no matter how big the state's population. The number of representatives, however, would depend on each state's population. Both parts of Congress had to agree on a law in order to pass it. The Connecticut Compromise became a basic part of the United States government.

PEOPLE

Prudence Crandall (1803-1890) was a schoolteacher who fought for African American rights. She opened a school for girls in 1831 in Canterbury, Connecticut. The school thrived until 1833. That year, Crandall admitted Sarah Harris. She was an African American. The townspeople objected and tried to close the school. All the white children left. Crandall kept the school open and taught other African American girls. Crandall was arrested for breaking Connecticut law. She was released, but further violence against the school forced her to close it in 1834.

The bravery and determination of Crandall and her students caused Connecticut laws to change. By 1838, African Americans were allowed an eduction in the state. In 1995, Connecticut honored Crandall by naming her the official state heroine. There is a statue of her and a student in the state capitol building in Hartford.

Nathan Hale (1755-1776) was a schoolteacher and Revolutionary War hero. He was born in Coventry, Connecticut, and attended Yale College in New Haven. In 1775, he volunteered to fight for America's independence from Great Britain. He became a first lieutenant in the 7th Connecticut Regiment of the Continental Army. In 1776, the young schoolteacher volunteered to spy on British military forces in New York. He was captured behind enemy lines and sentenced to hang. His final words were reportedly, "I only regret that I have but one life to lose for my country." Hale's bravery and tragic death inspired other patriots to fight for their country's independence. In 1985, Connecticut made Hale the state's official state hero.

Harriet Beecher Stowe (1811-1896) was an author and abolitionist who wanted to end slavery. In 1852, her book *Uncle Tom's Cabin* was published. It told the tragic story of slavery in the South. It became one of the most popular books in the world. In its first year, it sold more than 300,000 copies, which was a smash best seller for its time. It went on to sell millions. Although the book included many stereotypes about African Americans, it raised awareness about the evils of slavery. It fueled anti-slavery feelings leading up to the Civil War. Stowe was born in Litchfield, Connecticut.

Katharine Hepburn (1907-2003) was a popular actress of both stage and screen. She appeared in more than 40 films and dozens of stage plays. The American Film Institute called her one of the greatest Hollywood stars of all time. Hepburn was nominated 12 times for an Academy Award. She won four Oscars for Best Actress. Her most popular films included *The African Queen*, *The Lion in Winter*, and *On Golden Pond*. Hepburn was born in Fenwick, Connecticut.

CITIES

Bridgeport is Connecticut's most populous city. It is home to 147,612 people. It is in the southwest corner of the state, along the coast of Long Island Sound. Pequannock Native Americans first settled the area. In the 1640s, European settlers arrived. They were attracted to the deep harbor that provided shelter for shipbuilding and whaling vessels. Bridgeport was incorporated in 1821. As the city grew, many immigrants came to work in factories. Today, Bridgeport is known for manufacturing, banking, and health care. There are many shoreline parks. The city is also home to the University of Bridgeport and the Housatonic Museum of Art.

Hartford is the capital of Connecticut. It is in
the center of the state, along the banks of the Connecticut River.
The Native American Sicaog tribe lived here before Europeans arrived.
Dutch fur traders came to the area in the early 1600s. Today, Hartford
is Connecticut's fourth-largest city. It has a population 124,705. Several
major insurance companies have their headquarters in Hartford, making
it "The Insurance Capital of the World." There are many wealthy
businesses in Hartford, but there are also poor areas. Parts of the city are
diverse and historic. Some neighborhoods have ethnic flavors, including
Italian, African American, and Caribbean. Hartford is home to several
colleges, including Trinity College and the University of Hartford.

New Haven has a population of 130,282. It is the second-most populous city in Connecticut. It is located along the shores of Long Island Sound, at New Haven Harbor. The city began as a collection of English Puritan settlements in the early 1600s. It joined the Connecticut Colony in 1664. New Haven grew in importance because of its deepwater port and its many manufacturing companies. Today, the city's downtown bustles with shops, restaurants, and outdoor activities. The city is also home to Ivy League Yale University, which was established in 1701.

Stamford, with a population of 128,278, is Connecticut's third-most populous city. It is located on the state's southwestern panhandle. Many large corporations make their home in Stamford, including UBS, Pitney Bowes, and Tasty Bite. The city's population is diverse, young, and educated. Many people commute to work in nearby New York City, New York.

Waterbury is nicknamed "The Brass City." At one time, the city was the top producer of brass products. Its many factories also produce clocks, watches, and pewter products. It is located along the banks of the Naugatuck River, southwest of Hartford. Waterbury has a population of 109,307, making it the fifth-largest city in Connecticut.

TRANSPORTATION

Early in Connecticut's history, people and goods were carried by ship from the colony's seaports along Long Island Sound. Today, ferries shuttle passengers between Connecticut and New York or Rhode Island.

In the 1800s, railroads helped Connecticut grow by moving farm products and factory goods to other states. When roads were built for automobiles in the 1930s, railroads became less important. However, many Connecticut residents work in nearby New York City, New York, or Boston, Massachusetts. To avoid traffic jams, they prefer to ride Amtrak commuter trains that travel through the state.

Ferries regularly shuttle passengers and vehicles across Long Island Sound.

Connecticut has about 21,474 miles (34,559 km) of public roadways. Busy Interstate 95 runs southwest and northeast along the Long Island Sound coast. Interstate 91 goes north from the coast, through Hartford, and into neighboring Massachusetts. Several other interstate and state highways crisscross Connecticut.

There are more than 115 airports in Connecticut. Most of them are small. The busiest is Bradley International Airport near the capital of Hartford. It handles nearly 5.9 million passengers each year. Other busy airports in Connecticut include Tweed New Haven Regional Airport, Danielson Airport, Danbury Municipal Airport, Groton-New London Airport, Hartford-Brainard Airport, Waterbury-Oxford Airport, and Windham Airport.

Bradley International Airport is called the "Gateway to New England."

NATURAL
RESOURCES

About 60 percent of Connecticut is forested. This amounts to roughly 1.8 million acres (728,434 ha) of land. Most of it is privately owned. Oak and hickory trees make up about 72 percent of the woodlands. Forests are harvested to make items such as furniture, paper, and Christmas trees. Connecticut forests generate about $3.4 billion of income annually.

During the 1700s, iron and copper were mined from Connecticut's crust. Those mines have long been closed. Today, the most important mining products include sand, gravel, crushed stone, and gemstones such as garnets and topaz.

Jones Family Farms in Shelton, Connecticut, has 200 acres (81 ha) of Christmas trees, as well as other seasonal crops.

Commercial oyster fishermen with their haul from Long Island Sound, off Norwalk, Connecticut.

There are almost 6,000 farms in Connecticut. They occupy 436,000 acres (176,443 ha) of land. The state's soil was formed by glaciers long ago. The richest soil is along the Connecticut River Valley. Top crops include apples, peaches, pears, tobacco, and corn. Dairy cows and chickens are also important. Agriculture adds more than $4.5 billion to the state's economy each year.

Commercial fishing is an important part of Connecticut's economy and heritage. Species pulled from Long Island Sound and the Atlantic Ocean include sea scallops, clams, oysters, silver hake, squid, lobsters, butterfish, flounder, and monkfish.

NATURAL RESOURCES

INDUSTRY

The three biggest industries in Connecticut are insurance, finance, and real estate. Together, they account for almost one-third of the state's economy. Connecticut is called "The Insurance State." After the Revolutionary War, businesses began insuring ship cargoes. They also offered fire insurance. The insurance companies eventually grew and branched out. They insured not only ships, but all sorts of things, such as homes and autos. Today, Connecticut has more than 70 insurance companies. Many are located in the state capital of Hartford.

Tourism is a growing industry that provides thousands of jobs for Connecticut citizens. Visitors enjoy the state's historic sites, scenic countryside, and Long Island Sound resorts. More than 22 million tourists come to Connecticut each year, adding more than $14 billion to the state's economy.

Tourists visit Connecticut's Mystic Seaport. The shops and maritime museum surround a restored tall ship. The iron-hulled Joseph Conrad *training ship sits dockside.*

Mystic Seaport in Mystic, Connecticut

Sikorsky Aircraft builds helicopters in Stratford, Connecticut.

Manufacturing is a big part of Connecticut's economy. It developed early in the state's history. Fast rivers were used to power factories. Today, Connecticut companies produce machinery, electronics, chemical products, firearms, and many other kinds of goods. The state's biggest manufacturing plant is in Stratford, where Sikorsky Aircraft makes helicopters. In the city of Groton, General Dynamics Electric Boat builds U.S. Navy submarines.

General Dynamics Electric Boat builds U.S. Navy submarines in Groton, Connecticut.

SPORTS

Connecticut has no men's professional major league sports teams. However, the state hosts the Connecticut Sun, which plays in the Women's National Basketball Association. The Sun plays home games in Uncasville. The Connecticut Whale began playing in the National Women's Hockey League during the 2015-16 season. Connecticut also has several minor league teams, including the Bridgeport Sound Tigers and Hartford Wolf Pack (ice hockey), the New Britain Rock Cats (baseball), and the New England Black Wolves (lacrosse). The sport of lacrosse has grown very popular in the state. It began as a game played by Native Americans.

College sports are big in Connecticut. The University of Connecticut men's and women's basketball programs are especially popular. The women's UConn Huskies basketball team has won 10 NCAA Division I national championships as of 2015.

Fishing is a popular activity in Connecticut's streams and rivers.

Connecticut is filled with outdoor recreational activities. All along the Long Island Sound coastline, people enjoy boating and fishing. The state's dense forests are great for hunting, wildlife watching, camping, or simply strolling through the woods. Connecticut has 102 state parks, forests, and wildlife areas. Popular Hammonasset Beach State Park, near the town of Madison, includes more than two miles (3 km) of shoreline along the coast of Long Island Sound. It is Connecticut's largest public beach park.

SPORTS

ENTERTAINMENT

Connecticut is filled with interesting museums, art galleries, theaters, and music halls. In New Haven, Yale University is home to the Yale Peabody Museum of Natural History. It features exhibits on ancient Egypt, birds, geology, and dinosaurs. Also at Yale is the Wadsworth Atheneum. Founded in 1842, it is the oldest free public art museum in the country.

Goodspeed Opera House

The Goodspeed Opera House in East Haddam is a Victorian-style house built along the Connecticut River in 1876. In New Haven, the Long Wharf Theatre is a top regional playhouse that produces classic plays and musicals. Also in New Haven is the Yale Repertory Theatre.

Lake Compounce, in Bristol, is the nation's oldest continuously operated amusement park. Started in 1846, it features thrill rides, a beach, and Crocodile Cove, Connecticut's largest water park. Boulder Dash was voted the "best wooden roller coaster in the world" in 2015.

The Mystic Aquarium features New England's only beluga whales. In Stingray Bay swim Atlantic, southern, and cownose rays and a green sea turtle named Charlotte.

Mystic Seaport, in the village of Mystic, is a maritime museum and living history center. It has many historic ships and buildings that recreate an 1800s-era sea village. Mystic is also home to the Mystic Aquarium & Institute for Exploration. Opened in 1973, it is part research center and part tourist attraction. It features fish, marine mammals, and ocean exploration exhibits.

TIMELINE

1614—Dutch explorer Adriaen Block sails up the Connecticut River.

1636—A group of colonists led by Thomas Hooker moves into the area, creating a permanent English settlement near Hartford.

1636–1637—A violent war erupts between New England settlers and the Pequot tribe. Many Pequot die or are captured and sold into slavery.

1639—Connecticut adopts the Fundamental Orders, giving the colonists limited self-rule.

1775–1783—Connecticut sends thousands of men to fight against Great Britain in the Revolutionary War.

1788—Connecticut becomes the fifth state.

1848—Connecticut abolishes slavery.

1861–1865—Connecticut supports the Union during the American Civil War.

1917–1918—Factories in Connecticut make military supplies to support the troops during World War I.

1929—The Great Depression begins. Many people in Connecticut are without jobs.

1941–1945—Connecticut sends thousands of soldiers to fight during World War II. Submarines, airplane parts, and other military supplies made in Connecticut help the United States.

2004—University of Connecticut Huskies men's and women's basketball teams both win NCAA National Championship titles.

2012—The nation is shocked when 20 children and 6 staff are killed in a mass shooting at Sandy Hook Elementary School in Newtown, Connecticut.

2013-2014—After more than 5 years of repairs, the historic *Charles W. Morgan* whaling ship is relaunched at Mystic Seaport on July 21, 2013. Originally built in 1841, the museum ship sailed on her 38th voyage in 2014.

GLOSSARY

COLONY

A group of people who settle in a distant territory but remain citizens of their native country.

COMMUTER

A person who lives in one place and travels to work in another place.

CONFEDERACY

The Southern states of Alabama, Arkansas, Florida, Georgia, Louisiana, Mississippi, North Carolina, South Carolina, Tennessee, Texas, and Virginia. These states broke away from the United States during the Civil War and formed their own country known as the Confederate States of America, or simply the Confederacy.

FOUNDING FATHERS

The representatives from the 13 British colonies in North America who were leaders during the American Revolution. They also either signed the Declaration of Independence in 1776 or helped draft the United States Constitution in 1787.

FUNDAMENTAL ORDERS

A document that brought individual cities and villages together to form one unit. It functioned like a constitution to unite the people.

LONG ISLAND SOUND

A body of water that is part of the Atlantic Ocean. The sound is between Connecticut and New York's Long Island.

MASSACHUSETTS BAY COLONY

An English colony, first settled by a group of Puritans in 1630, which later became the state of Massachusetts.

NEW ENGLAND

An area in the northeast United States. It consists of the states of Maine, Vermont, New Hampshire, Massachusetts, Rhode Island, and Connecticut.

NUTMEG

A valuable food spice used in cooking. The egg-shaped seeds come from a tropical tree.

PANHANDLE

An area of land that juts out from the rest of the state. In Connecticut, there is a panhandle in the very southwest corner of the state.

PURITANS

A religious group of the 16th and 17th century. They were English Protestants who wanted to "purify" the Church of England. They could be very strict in how they practiced Christianity. Many left England to seek religious freedom in North America.

WORLD WAR II

A conflict that was fought from 1939 to 1945, involving countries around the world. The United States entered the war after Japan bombed the American naval base at Pearl Harbor, in Oahu, Hawaii, on December 7, 1941.

INDEX